THE JOHN CALVIN McNAIR LECTURES

A WORKING FAITH

A WORKING FAITH

BY

CHARLES REYNOLDS BROWN
Dean of the Yale Divinity School

CHAPEL HILL
THE UNIVERSITY OF NORTH CAROLINA PRESS
LONDON: HUMPHREY MILFORD
OXFORD UNIVERSITY PRESS
1926

Copyright, 1926, By
THE UNIVERSITY OF NORTH CAROLINA PRESS

PRESSES OF
EDWARDS & BROUGHTON COMPANY
RALEIGH

THE McNAIR LECTURES

The John Calvin McNair Lectures were founded through a bequest made by Rev. John Calvin McNair, of the class of 1849, which became available to the University in 1906. The extract from the will referring to the foundation is as follows:

"As soon as the interest accruing thereon shall by said Trustees be deemed sufficient they shall employ some able scientific gentleman to deliver before the students then in attendance at said University, a course of lectures, the object of which lectures shall be to show the mutual bearing of science and theology upon each other, and to prove the existence of attributes (as far as may be) of God from nature. The lectures, which must be prepared by a member of some one of the evangelic denominations of Christians, must be published within twelve months after delivery, either in pamphlet or book form."

PREFACE

When the invitation to deliver the McNair Lectures at the University of North Carolina was first extended to me, that phrase in the wording of the Foundation which suggests that they shall have to do with "the mutual bearing of science and theology upon each other" discouraged me from accepting. I have not had a scientific training, and if I should undertake to deal with any branch of modern science in its bearing upon religion, I should be dismayed by such a task.

I was assured, however, that this provision had been construed somewhat broadly and generously so that men of Christian faith could, within the borders of their own fields of study, present discussions bearing directly upon the great interest of religion. I understand that in the alternate years the appointment is offered to scholars whose work has been directly in some branch of science. Then on the other years the subject of religious faith has been approached from different angles.

This is one of the "off years" and I am generously permitted to bring a contribution from "my own line of goods," which is religion. I seek to indicate here some of the chief elements which enter into an ordinary working faith. Naturally I have had in mind primarily the religious thinking of undergraduates, who are making those inevitable readjustments, which take place when we are recasting the beliefs which we have carried along from the earlier years in the light of expanding knowledge consequent upon our studies in history, in philosophy, and in science.

I have retained here the more simple and direct forms of oral address with an occasional bit of personal appeal as best suited to the purpose for which the lectures were prepared.

I wish to thank The Century Company for permission to use several paragraphs from my book, *These Twelve*, published by them, which I have inserted here in the first of these lectures. I would also thank the Yale University Press for their courtesy in allowing me to use a portion of the story about "The Man on the Jericho Road" from my book, *Where Do You Live?* which I have introduced in the third lecture as illustrating the value of right motive.

For the honor of this appointment, for the many courtesies I received from the President and from other members of the Faculty, on the occasion of my visit to the University of North Carolina, and for the cordial response of the students, I shall be ever deeply grateful.

CHARLES R. BROWN.

Yale University
June 1926

CONTENTS

I.	What We Live By . . .	1
II.	What Does It Mean to Be a Christian?	44
III.	What Value Has Right Motive?	88

A WORKING FAITH

I

WHAT WE LIVE BY

How easy it is to load up with a lot of excess baggage! Mere luggage to be carried along which adds nothing to the pleasure or the profit of the trip! Superfluous things which have long since become liabilities rather than assets!

We purchase articles of furniture and bric-a-brac and place them in our homes. They may contribute nothing to the comfort or the beauty of those homes. They merely take up room which otherwise we might be using ourselves. We leave them there simply because they have been there a long time. Housekeepers are uniformly conservative. It is well for a family to move now and then from North Carolina to California, or from California to Connecticut, just to get rid of some of this excess baggage.

We purchase books and place them on our shelves—books which were never worth buying, books scarcely worth reading. We leave them there just because they have been there a long time. I suppose every family represented here which has five hundred books in the home, has at least two hundred which have not been opened for the last ten years and will not be opened for the next twenty. They are merely excess baggage to be carried along. It would be good to have the express wagon back up to the door and haul them away to the second-hand bookstore or to the furnace. They would burn well because they are so dry.

In like manner the individual may load up with a lot of habits, beliefs, ideas which add nothing to the zest and relish of life. They open up no new sources of motive and stimulus for right action. They are just so much baggage to be carried along. The man leaves them there in his head and in his heart just because they have been there a long time. It is good for an individual to move now and then intellectually and spiritually just to get rid of some of this excess baggage.

What We Live By 3

But there are certain interests which are not in that class. They are vital, usable, essential. We cannot get on without them. They are the things we live by.

There was an ancient singer once who summed up his whole philosophy of life in a single sentence which is familiar no doubt to most of you. "Trust in the Lord and do good, so shalt thou dwell in the land and verily thou shalt be fed." He touched there on four of the great main interests in human life. Religious faith,—"trust in the Lord!" Humane service,—"do good!" Political stability,—"so shalt thou dwell in the land!" Economic security,—"verily thou shalt be fed!"

Faith and love, citizenship and employment—they may not entirely cover the ground but, taken with all their natural implications, they cover a good, large share of it. This ancient singer would have them all brought under the power of intelligent purpose and moral consecration. Let me discuss them with you in order as the things we live by.

The use we make of them has a very direct bearing on what I have called "A Working Faith."

First, religious faith—"trust in the Lord!" The man showed his wisdom by putting first that which is first. He would have every man faced right at the start. He would have him orient himself correctly. Let him seek first the kingdom of God, the rule of the divine spirit in his own heart, so that all the other things requisite for right living might be added in their proper order.

"Trust in the Lord"—it lies at the basis of all that is best in personal character and in social well-being. It is the way to begin. No man has learned the ABC's of right living until he has learned to do just that.

Some one said to Frederick W. H. Myers, the English philosopher, "If you could ask the Sphinx but a single question and be sure of an answer, what would it be?" Quick as a flash his reply came back—"Is the universe friendly?"

Is the sum total of things on our side or against us or merely indifferent like the weather? Is the universe on the whole friendly? The psalmist believed that the universe is friendly to right living. "Trust in the Lord"—you may! If you would attain to that which is best, you must.

It has to do with what we call "religion." I shall use that term in these lectures in its broader sense as including the religion of the Protestant, the Catholic, the Hebrew, the religion of honest and devout men everywhere. Wherever you find a conscious, personal bearing toward a being conceived of as divine and the expression of that bearing in worship and in conduct ordered with reference to what is believed to be the will of that divine being, there you have religion. And no other single interest can be named which has entered so widely, so continuously, so powerfully into the renewal of man's moral nature, into the shaping of his ultimate ideals, and into the formation of personal character, as that sense of contact between the human and the divine which we call religion.

It is an interest which endures. Some things last for a season like bobbed hair and the latest bit of current slang. Some things last for a decade or two and then they are gone. Some things last for a century. "Our little systems have their day, they have their day and cease to be." Religion lasts from generation to generation, from age to age.

It has been here from the very beginning. Cities without walls, cities without libraries, cities without art galleries, cities without music, but never a city, the historians tell us, without its places of worship! Religion has been with us from the beginning and it will be here until time is no more. Men seek eternally for the sense of fellowship and contact with Him who is above all and through all and in us all.

The Bible has been on the market for more than eighteen centuries and through all those hundreds of years it has been "the best seller." Over six millions of copies of this book were printed and sold during the last year. Two publishing houses alone, one in this country and one in Great Britain—I am taking these figures from the *Encyclopedia Brittanica,* which is fairly reliable in its statistics— have printed and sold more than seven hundred millions of copies of the Bible. It will continue to sell as long as men can read. It owes its currency and its permanency in the world of human interest to the fact that it deals with religion. There will never come a time when men and women do not trust in the Lord and find in that trust guidance, reinforcement, and inspiration for right living.

Men have argued themselves hoarse over the question as to whether or not Abraham Lincoln was a religious man. It is significant that the question has never been raised as to whether General Robert E. Lee was a religious man. Every one who knew him or who knew about him felt sure that he was a high-minded Christian gentleman who gave his fine abilities to the service of those causes which he esteemed just and right. But there has been great disagreement over the question as to whether Abraham Lincoln could be called a religious man.

It all depends on what you mean by being religious. He was not a member of any church. I do not know that he was ever baptized. I am not sure that he ever partook of the sacrament of the Lord's Supper. He used to say, however, "If any church would inscribe above its altars as the sole condition for membership those two great words of the Saviour, 'Thou shalt love the Lord thy God with all thy heart; thou shalt love thy neighbor as thyself' that church would I join." He could be accommodated today.

I like to remember, however, that when he was leaving Springfield, Illinois, for the city of Washington to take up the duties of the Presidency, he gave a little farewell address to the friends and neighbors who gathered at the railroad station to see him off, closing with these words, "I go to take up a hard task not knowing whether I shall ever return." He never did return except in his casket. "But trusting in Him who can go with me and remain here with you and be everywhere for good, let us hope that at last all may be well."

The closing words of his second Inaugural have become classic: "Fondly do we hope, fervently do we pray that this mighty scourge of war may speedily pass. But if it should be decreed that it continue until all the wealth heaped up by the bondsman's unrequited toil should be sunk and until every drop of blood drawn by the lash should be paid for by another drop drawn by the sword, as it was said three thousand years ago, so still it must be said, 'The judgments of the Lord are true and righteous altogether.'"

The man who could say that and feel it and live it was surely a religious man. Trust in the Lord. It lies at the basis of all that is best. It is the first great main interest by which men live.

In the second place humane service—"Do good." You can have morality of a certain type without religion. There are men like Felix Adler of New York who cannot find it in their hearts to believe in God or to lift up holy hands in prayer or to cherish the hope of a future life, who nevertheless are striving with all their might to do justly, to love mercy, and to make the world a better place by the way they order their own conduct.

We wish that they had a more satisfactory philosophy of life. We crave for them the added motive and stimulus which comes from faith in a world unseen. But even so, we rejoice in their determination to believe that God or no God, truth is better than falsehood, kindliness is better than selfishness and cruelty, clean living is better than lust. We rejoice in their determination to order their lives in harmony with these principles. "Be good," they say, "and do good, for this is the law and the prophets for us." It is all they have and it is not to be despised. You can have a certain measure of morality without religion.

But you cannot have religion without morality. If it is without morality, it is not real religion. You can have forms and ceremonies; you can have theological opinions and beliefs; you can have emotional upheavals and mystical stirrings, without morality. But these are not religion—they are only means which religion may use to gain its ends.

Religion is life. It is the living of the life of a child of God by the grace God gives. And that life must utter itself steadily in doing good. All religious forms and beliefs which do not speedily find expression in fair dealing, in kindly speech, in unselfish action, have no more value than sounding brass and tinkling cymbal. The natural, inevitable fruits of the religious spirit are love, joy, peace, patience, gentleness, goodness, faithfulness, mildness, self-control. Trust in the Lord and let that sublime trust find expression in doing good.

It was the glory of the Hebrew race that early in their history they laid firm hold on that principle. The God in whom they put their trust was not a God of etiquette intent mainly upon certain polite forms of deference to himself. He was not a God who played favorites, loving the Jews because they were Jews and hating the other nations because they were not. He was a God of character, a covenant making and a covenant keeping God, a God upon whose word they could rely. He was interested supremely in righteousness and would be satisfied with nothing less.

When those Israelites were encamped at Mt. Sinai, they saw a huge, rugged mountain rising abruptly out of the plain. Black clouds rested upon it as if some heavenly visitant had come down robed in thick darkness. When the storm broke, the flash of the lightning was to their primitive minds like a momentary glimpse of that divine glory which no man could see and live. The roar of the thunder was to them like the sound of a superhuman voice.

But all this was mere stage play; it was only the setting of the scene. The significant fact is to be found in what

What We Live By 13

they came to believe that the voice had said. "Have no other Gods before me! Honor thy father and thy mother! Thou shalt not kill nor steal nor commit adultery, nor bear false witness!" Life and purity, truth and property, family peace and personal reputation were all sacred in the eyes of the Deity whose voice they heard; and those interests must be sacred also in the eyes of his people. Trust in the Lord and show that trust by living uprightly, unselfishly, usefully!

Say it with deeds! It cannot be so well said in any other way. "Not every one that saith unto me, Lord, Lord, shall enter the kingdom of heaven, but he that doeth the will of my Father who is in heaven." "He that heareth these sayings of mine and doeth them, I will liken unto a wise man who built his house upon a rock."

I was reading a letter several years ago written by the great Hindu poet Tagore. He was writing to a young English clergyman who had just arrived in India as a missionary—and this is the substance of what he wrote.

"Do not be forever just preaching your doctrine,—give yourself in kindly sacrificial service. Your object in coming to India, you say, is to make men like Jesus Christ. This will be accomplished mainly by self-sacrifice and in personal ministry to human need. Preaching is not sacrifice. It may be a form of self-indulgence more dangerous than any kind of material luxury. Men are often tempted to think that they have been doing their duty when they were merely talking about it. And the best preaching of all is done by going about doing good."

And all this from a man who does not call himself a Christian—he is a Hindu! But how it resembles that word of the Master, "If ye know these things, happy are ye if ye do them." "In him was life and the life was the light of men." It is for men to let their light so shine in kindly service that other men may see and find their way into life eternal.

How many of you are familiar with the story of Bishop Welcome? His name fitted him; it grew right out of him like his hair. Wherever he went he was just that—he was "welcome." When he was first made a bishop he found that the bishop's palace had in it sixty splendid rooms while the little town hospital across the street had only six. He visited the hospital first. He went about among the sick people uttering words of cheer and hope, offering prayer with some of those who were more seriously ill. When he had finished his round, he came to the head physician and said to him, "Your beds are too close together. Your patients have not sufficient air. They are not getting well as fast as they should."

"You are quite right," replied the physician, "but what can we do—we have no more room."

"It is perfectly clear to me," said the bishop, "that they have gotten these houses mixed up. You have my house and I have yours. Restore me my own! Your place is across the street."

He then had all the sick people moved over into the bishop's palace with its sixty splendid rooms and he lived for the rest of his days in the little one story, six room cottage. That interested the people of the diocese. They had never seen it on that fashion before. That was not just their idea of bishops.

It was said of Bishop Welcome that so long as he had any money in his pockets he went about visiting the poor of the diocese to help them. When his money was all gone, then he visited the rich to ask them for more money to help the poor.

He announced one Sunday from his pulpit that the following week he intended to go up into the mountains to visit some shepherds who were keeping their flocks in an out of the way place, to tell them about the goodness of God and to give them the holy sacrament. The mountains at that time were infested with brigands. The people were afraid to travel there. The Mayor of the city called upon him that afternoon to protest against his going. "It would be dangerous," the Mayor said. "You would need an escort of soldiers, and even then you would be imperiling their lives as well as your own."

"For that reason," the Bishop replied, "I shall go without an escort."

"Alone?"

"Alone."

"They will rob you."

"I have nothing."

"They will kill you."

"A harmless old priest passing along muttering his prayers? What good would that do them?"

"Well, what would you do if you met the brigands?"

"Ah," said the Bishop, "I am glad you thought of that! They too must need to hear about the goodness of God. I would tell them about the goodness of God and then I would ask them for alms for my poor."

The Mayor saw that he could not do anything with a man like that. He too had never seen it on that fashion before.

The next morning the bishop set out for the mountains with one small boy who had offered to go with him and show him the way. He found the shepherds and spent the week with them, preaching to them the gospel and administering to them the holy communion for which they were profoundly grateful. While he was there a great treasure of gold and silver and precious stones was sent to him with this inscription pinned upon it,—"To Bishop Welcome. From Cravatte."

Cravatte was the ring leader of the brigands.

When the Bishop returned and was showing his treasure to the curate, before it was converted into money to be used for the needs of the diocese, he said to him "To those who are satisfied with little, God sends much."

"God," replied the curate, "or the devil?"

The bishop looked at him long and earnestly and said, "God."

The Bishop went once to call on an old man who was supposed to be an infidel. The old man lived by himself in a lonely place an hour's walk from the town. He was said to be dying. When the Bishop entered, the old man raised his head and said, "Who are you?"

"My name is Welcome."

"Then you are my bishop," the man replied with a quizzical look.

"Possibly. I am glad to find that you do not seem to be seriously ill."

"I shall soon be better," the man replied. "In three hours I shall be dead. Yesterday my feet were cold. Now the cold has reached my knees. I can feel it approaching my waist. When it touches the heart, all will be over. What a beautiful sunset we are to have," he added, turning his face to the west.

Then the two men talked together simply and naturally for two hours while the shadows fell around them. And the dying man who had been without faith or hope or love found a strange, sweet, deep sense of peace in the presence and sympathy of this saint of God.

At last he said, "I am eighty-six years old and I am about to die. What have you come to ask of me?"

"Your blessing," said the Bishop as he fell upon his knees. He prayed silently, and when he raised his head the spirit of the old man had returned to Him who gave it.

The Bishop went home deeply absorbed in thought. He spent the whole night in prayer. The next day when some of the villagers tried to gossip with him about the death of the old man who had been regarded as an unbeliever, the Bishop shook his head and silently pointed toward heaven.

The bishop never wrote any books. He never preached any eloquent sermons. He never stood at the head of any conspicuous religious movement. But it was the universal testimony that no man in that whole region had done more to make the religion of Christ effective than this man who went about doing good.

The Master of all the higher values in life made bold one day to draw a picture of the final judgment when men would be set off on the right hand or the left of the divine favor, even as a shepherd divides the sheep from the goats. It is generally regarded as one of the most solemn and significant passages in all his teaching.

The principle upon which that division would be made as he saw it is highly significant. The fate of the individual in that unseen world would not turn upon the question of his membership in this organization or in that; it would not turn upon his acceptance of this set of theological beliefs or that; it would not turn upon his having performed or having failed to perform certain sacred rites and ceremonies. The Master drew a picture of the hungry, the naked, the sick, the imprisoned, as outstanding types of the world's need. With eager, active sympathy, he identified himself with all that pain and distress. "I was hungry; I was naked; I was sick and in prison!"

Then he said that a man's eternal destiny would depend upon his having rendered or having failed to render kindly, efficient service to that human need. "Inasmuch as ye did it or did it not to the least of these, you will inherit the reward prepared for you or you will depart into age-long penalty for your cold hearted selfishness." He knew what human life was and needed not that any should tell him. He felt that the presence or the absence of that kindly spirit in the heart was decisive. "Trust in the Lord and do good"— that is the second great main interest by which we live.

In the third place, political stability— "so shalt thou dwell in the land." How strange it is that many upright people look upon political life as an unclean thing! Whenever the word "politics" is mentioned they look as if something nauseating had been offered them. They seem to think that there is an unsavory quality about all these civic interests.

They never got that idea here in the Bible. "The powers that be," said one who was himself a Roman citizen, free born and proud of the fact—"The powers that be are ordained of God."

"The powers that be,'—mayors, governors, presidents, aldermen, legislators, congressmen, policemen, sheriffs, soldiers—all these are ordained of God for the high ends of order and justice. Good government is a necessary item in the divine program. Good citizenship is as much a part of a Christian's duty as the saying of his prayers. "Render unto Caesar the things which are Caesar's," even as you render unto God the things that are His.

Yet straight in the face of all that teaching of Scripture and of common sense, you will find a lot of people who think that if they pay their taxes regularly and obey the laws,—most of them, making room for certain exceptions having to do with the Eighteenth Amendment and the regulation of traffic,—and stand ready to sing the "Star Spangled Banner" and "America" lustily upon occasion,—if they do these things they must be good citizens.

But if you were to suggest to any one of them that he should neglect his private business or subject himself to serious personal inconvenience in order to hold public office or to engage actively in civic affairs, he would look at you as if it were a thing almost too preposterous to be talked about. They want "good government"—of course they want good government. They want protection for their lives and property and investments, at a minimum cost in the matter of taxation, but they also want to be left alone to feather their own nests, making them soft and warm, and then be allowed to get in and lie down and be comfortable, leaving the disagreeable task of attending caucuses and primaries, of looking after ward organizations and political conventions to somebody else. They may be very respectable people but they are political slackers.

Several years ago in three of our most prominent American cities three professional politicians who had already shown themselves woefully inefficient, (not to put it more strongly), in the very offices to which they aspired, were triumphantly reëlected by handsome majorities. The good citizens read the results of the election the next morning at their breakfast tables with dismay. "How in the world did those fellows get in again?" they said. And they also said other things which it might not be proper for me to repeat, being a clergyman.

They had themselves to thank for it. It developed later that tens of thousands of them, men and women alike, especially in the sections of those cities where the more intelligent and prosperous people resided, did not even take sufficient interest in the matter to register and vote. They got exactly what was coming to them and so long as that political apathy prevails to such an extent among the more intelligent and prosperous classes in our American cities, they will continue to get what is coming to them.

Here in the oldest book in the Bible, the book of Judges, some shrewd old chap wrote a short story which ought to be read at least once a year in every pulpit in the land, Protestant, Catholic, and Hebrew. It is known as "the Parable of Jotham." The trees met, you remember, to elect a king. They asked the fig tree "to stand," as they say in England, or "to run" for office as we say in our more restless country. The fig tree declined. It said, "No, I cannot neglect my business of producing figs in order to hold public office. My business is too sweet."

They asked the olive tree to stand. But the olive tree declined. It said, "No, I cannot neglect my business of producing ripe olives and olive oil in order to hold public office. My business is too fat."

They asked the vine to stand but the vine declined. It said, "No, I cannot neglect my business of producing grapes and wine, which makes glad the hearts of men, in order to hold public office. My business is too delightful and exhilarating."

All the better members of the tree kingdom declined. Then in default of any better material a poor old, of-no-account bramble, who was not producing

What We Live By 27

anything, came forward and said that if the office of king was going begging, he would be willing to serve. The trees therefore elected the bramble and he waved to and fro over the trees, as king.

Hear therefore the Parable of the Trees! It might have been written a few years ago in Boston or in New York or in Chicago. We find brambles in the City Hall. We find brambles in the state legislature. We sometimes find what the chemist would call "traces" of the bramble even in Congress. We find them there chiefly because of the reluctance of better men to show an active interest in civic affairs.

The free institutions of a republic will not run themselves any better than any other set of political institutions. They offer an opportunity—according to our political belief the very best of opportunities—for the high-minded, honest-hearted people to give political expression to their desires and determinations for the common good. Sitting down and piously reading the Declaration of Independence or a weekly copy of the *Nation* or singing "America" is not good citizenship any more than a woman sitting in a rocking chair reading her cookbook and humming "Home Sweet Home" is good housekeeping. The woman will have to give herself actively and intelligently to a great many plain and practical duties in order to make her house a home. In like manner true citizenship includes devotion to many a concrete task.

These "high-minded, honest-hearted people" must be on their job every day in the year and not merely on the morning after the election when they are voicing their indignation over an outcome which they, in all probability, did little or nothing to avert. If "government of the people, by the people and for the people," is not to "perish from the earth," then society will have to show itself able to select and place in power those best men, best in personal character, best in judgment, best in civic efficiency, whose right it is to rule. If the cause of democracy is not to go down in defeat under the weight of ignorance and indifference, then the general average of citizenship must be brought up to a higher level.

"Pray for the peace of Jerusalem!" Pray for the peace of Washington and for the peace of London and Paris and Berlin and Rome and Tokyo! "For there are set thrones of judgment!" There are centers of authority from which will radiate those forms of influence which will hasten or retard the coming of the kingdom of God on earth. It will advance or retard the reign of that spirit which is righteousness and peace and good will among men. Trust in the Lord and let that trust find expression in a more intelligent, conscientious, and active quality of citizenship. So shalt thou dwell in the land!

In the fourth place economic security—"verily thou shalt be fed!" Man does not live by bread alone, neither does he live without bread. He lives by all the great words which proceed out of the mind of God, faith, hope, love,—

food, clothing, shelter,—courage, aspiration, high resolve,—knowledge, beauty, affection. By all these men live.

The brain and heart are fed and sustained by a body which is of the earth earthy. The mental and spiritual development of the race must have some sort of secure physical basis. When we talk about "saving souls" and "the culture of souls," we are not to forget that the only "souls" we know anything about at present are souls which have the cheerful habit of living in bodies. And these bodies have to be fed, clothed, housed every day in the year. At the base of the Pyramid therefore, no matter how high it is to rise, there must be a sound economic life resting upon rightly ordered industry.

It was a man who lived in a very hot climate, a man who had not lived very long nor grown very tall, who once said that it was the curse of God that men were compelled to earn their bread by the sweat of their brows.

How little he knew! He was still in the primer—he had not gotten hold of the first reader as yet. Work is a blessing. Man was made for work. He finds himself through his work. He wins character and expresses it by doing square work and square work only. He adds cubits to his stature physically, mentally, morally, by doing whatever his hand or his head or his heart finds to do thoroughly and well.

It was the greatest of all the apostles who said to those people at Philippi, "Work out your own salvation!" Work it out! He knew full well that men will not be saved by sermons and sacraments on Sunday unless they are also being saved on the other six days of the week by the work they do, by the way they do it, by the spirit they put into it. Work is a blessing ordained of God for man's good.

You will find in every community a certain number of people who are going to the bad chiefly because they have nothing else to do. Some of them are going in limousines and some of them in Fords and some of them on foot. But they are all going.

They are unemployed. Some of them from choice. They have enough and to spare; they do not want to work; they desire only to roam about over the face of the earth and amuse themselves—and that is their ruination.

Some of them are unemployed from necessity. They are not specially gifted, either in hand or brain, and for certain periods of almost every year, they find themselves out of work.

Alas for them all! Except for the aged and the little children and the invalids, there is scarcely a sorrier fate than for a man or a woman to have nothing to do. For all the rest of us, work is a blessing and a divine necessity. Trust in the Lord and do some useful piece of work thoroughly and well as part of the daily program, and verily thou shalt be fed in body, mind, and heart.

However, it must be the work of a human being and not the work of a beast of burden. It must be the work of a self-respecting, aspiring human being and not the work which degrades and brutalizes. There are forms of toil which are cursed of God.

The Commission on Industrial Life appointed by the Federal Council of Churches some years ago found that in a certain well-known industry seventy-one per cent of the men were working at that time twelve hours a day for seven days in the week. When they changed from the day shift to the night shift they worked straight through the twenty-four hours. They found also that forty-three per cent of those employees were receiving less than the minimum wage named by a Federal Commission as the lowest amount on which an American family could be supported in decency.

When a man is working twelve hours a day seven days in the week, what kind of a husband is he when he comes home? What kind of a father? What kind of a neighbor? What kind of a citizen? You all know. The man has been sacrificed to a profit-making machine. The human values have gone down in defeat before the desire for gain. It is not enough to say of any industry that it is "making money"—it must also be making manhood and womanhood for those people whose lives and interests are bound up in that enterprise.

When we come to judge some phases of our modern industrial life, coal mining, steel making, the garment workers' industry, the textile workers, for example, by these more intelligent standards, we do not feel exactly like throwing up our hats. "We have followed too much the devices and desires of our own hearts, and have done those things which we ought not to have done."

We have put too much trust in certain well-worn maxims—they are so "well-worn" that they are worn out. "Pile on all the traffic will bear." "Buy in the cheapest market, sell in the dearest." "Look out for Number One. If you do not nobody will." "Follow ruthless competition, for competition is the life of trade." "Obey the spirit of an enlightened self-interest—if every man does that, it will result in the greatest good to the greatest number."

We have followed these maxims in the past, and in half the lands of earth they have produced a spirit of unrest, sullen and menacing. They have produced a spirit of unreason, wild and reckless, which sometimes throws principle and prudence to the winds and catches the nearest way to gain its ends. The spirit of selfishness and greed never has produced a social order fit to live in or one that would stand. It never will, because it is at war with certain fundamental instincts in our own hearts and it is at war with the will of God.

Why not try the Golden Rule in industry? We have already adopted it in family life. In our homes, the strong do not take the best of it because they are strong, leaving the fag ends to the weak. The strong bear the infirmities of the weak. The well people take care of the sick people. The grownups look out for the little people. The bread-winners and the love-makers pool their interests. In the family we do unto others as we would that others should do unto us.

We have adopted the Golden Rule in our friendships and in all the pleasant contacts of social life. You cannot build a friendship on the plan of piling on all the traffic will bear, or upon the principle of every man taking all that he can get and giving as little as he must. In all those relationships we do unto others as we would that others should do unto us.

Why not also in industry? Why should not every employer ask himself, "How would I like to be in my own employ? How would I like the conditions in this shop or this factory or this mine, for which I am responsible?" Why should not every employee ask himself, "Would I employ myself if I were the boss, responsible for the continuance and prosperity of this business? Is the use that I make of time, material, and tools, the use that I would like to see a man making of these things if he were working for me? Would I hire myself if I were responsible for the maintenance of this business?"

This attitude of mind and heart on the part of employers and employees would not solve all the problems of industry and usher in the millenium by a week from next Thursday. It would, however, enable us to take a long step forward toward a larger measure of industrial peace and prosperity.

"We are all members one of another" in an economic solidarity from which there is no escape. "If one member suffers, other members suffer with it." If one member prospers, it can only enjoy its largest measure of prosperity where that prosperity is shared by all the other members. "The head cannot say to the foot," the highest cannot say to the lowest nor the lowest to the highest, "I have no need of you." We are all members one of another.

The man possessed of five talents of organizing and administrative ability, standing therefore at the head of an industry, cannot say to the man of one talent who has only his muscle and his skill, "I have no need of you." The man of rare ability can only work out his plans through the coöperation of those men who stand in lower positions. The man possessed of only one talent, standing at the foot of the class, cannot say to the man possessed of five talents of organizing and administrative ability, "I have no need of you." We are all bound up together in an economic solidarity.

My head, for example, would scarcely have succeeded in reaching the lecture hall tonight without the help of my two feet. But if my two feet had insisted on coming alone without my head, you would not have had much of a lecture. The whole case for the division of labor and the diversity of operation is there suggested.

If two hands get on better and accomplish more when they act in coöperation, each one supplementing the action of the other; if two eyes are more efficient when they act together, each one focusing the image on its own retina in a common image rather than pulling apart in cross-eyed fashion; if two feet get on better when they move along in the same direction in coöperation rather than pulling apart in certain cross purposes; why not two men or two classes of men, employers and employees, or two races of men, white men and black men, or two nations of men, Americans and Japanese?

Is not that good arithmetic all the way through? We are all members one of another. We succeed best when we act together in friendliness and coöperation rather than when we pull apart in antagonism and strife. We stand or fall, we prosper or we perish, we advance or we recede as members of one great body.

The interests of the employer and the employee are not identical, nor are they antagonistic—they are reciprocal. The employer wants profits. He will not invest his capital, his time, his organizing, and administrative ability in any enterprise unless there is a fair chance for profit. But if he is a man of sense, he also wants a satisfied set of employees who are happy and responsive in their work rather than bitter and grudging. He knows that morale is as necessary in industry as it is in an army.

On the other hand, the employee wants good wages, reasonable hours, shop conditions which are satisfactory. But if he has any sense, he wants his employer to make money and prosper. He knows that unless his employer does prosper, the business will not continue and there will be no wages there for anybody. The interests of the employer and the employee are not identical but they are not antagonistic—they are reciprocal.

How often have you seen this! The employers in a certain industry undertake to force wages down below the point where they should have gone. Suppose they succeed. Then they find that a discontented, rebellious set of employees do not show a high average of productive effort. They also find that badly paid operatives do not buy goods. They see that they have destroyed an important part of their own market and have defeated their own ends by a policy of short-sighted selfishness.

In some other region, the labor unions undertake to force wages up unreasonably, to restrict output and to impose conditions which cripple industry. They succeed to such an extent that the employers are not willing to risk their capital, their time, and their efforts, under conditions which offer no reasonable prospect for profit. They therefore shut down the plants and the selfish, shortsighted employees find themselves walking the streets in search of jobs.

Here is the philosophy of life advocated by the greatest of the apostles. "Look not every one on his own things but every one also on the things of others." He was too wise to suggest that any man should disregard his own interests and look solely upon the interests of others. He would not try to make men too good to be true. Let every man look upon his own interests and also upon the interests of others as bound up with his own in that social solidarity which is as real as the power of gravitation which enfolds us all.

The Master also was too wise to say, "Thou shalt love thy neighbor but not thyself." He would have every man love himself and make the most possible of his own life as long as he did not interfere with any other man's chance to do the same thing for himself. The Master would make an intelligent self-regard the high standard to which neighborly regard for others might gradually measure up. "Thou shalt love thy neighbor as thyself."

This is the gospel for industry, as it is the gospel for all the interests of our common life. Trust in the Lord and let that trust find expression in looking also upon the interests of your fellows. So shall we all dwell in the land together and verily we shall be fed.

Here then is our work cut out for us and laid ready to our hands! Here are the great human interests which by the operation of a working faith are to be brought under the power of intelligent purpose and moral consecration! Faith and love, citizenship and employment! Religious faith and humane service, intelligent citizenship and rightly ordered economic life! "Trust in the Lord and do good, so shalt thou dwell in the land and verily thou shalt be fed!" These are the things men live by!

II

WHAT DOES IT MEAN TO BE A CHRISTIAN?

THERE was a time when hard and fast lines were drawn between the sheep and the goats. Here on the right hand were those who were Christians, here on the left were those who were not! The rough and ready evangelist would sometimes ask all the people in the congregation who were Christians to stand up, leaving those who were not quite ready to place that high appraisal upon themselves sitting down. "Here are the saved," he would say, "and here are the lost! Here are those who are going to heaven and here are those who are bound for the other place."

He was very sure about it. He made it all as definite and exact as if he had been putting all the blue-eyed people on one side of the church and all the brown-eyed people on the other side.

Now when the line was drawn and the division made on the basis of church membership, it was comparatively simple.

What Is a Christian? 45

For centuries there was only one church in the greater part of Christendom. You either belonged or you did not. You were either a member of the body of Christ by virtue of your standing in that one organization, or you were condemned as a rank outsider; and that was all there was about it.

They coined their conviction on that point into a clear-cut statement. *"Extra ecclesiam nulla salus,"* they said in their stately Latin. Outside of the church there is no salvation for anybody. And that was that!

But in these days we have more than a hundred different churches in this country alone. Methodists, Baptists, Presbyterians, Roman Catholics, Episcopalians, Lutherans, Congregationalists, Disciples, Unitarians, and all the rest! Which one of these many churches has the right of it? Are they all right? Are they all wrong but one—if so, which one? Who can say?

We are not quite so bigoted in these days as that Scotch clergyman was a generation ago. Two men, one a member of the Established Church, the other a member of the Free Kirk, were discussing the claims of their respective churches. The Free Churchman was the broader and the more genial man of the two. He finally said, "After all, I do not see that there is much difference between us when we come to the essentials."

"There is just one difference," the other man replied stiffly. "We will be saved and you will be damned." It would be almost impossible to find that attitude of mind today in any Protestant church. No single Protestant church is claiming that it has the truth, the whole truth, and nothing but the truth, while all the other churches are off the track.

When that line was drawn and the division between the sheep and the goats was made upon the basis of theological belief, the matter was comparatively simple. For centuries there were only three creeds which people generally knew anything about, the Apostles Creed, the Nicene Creed, and the Athanasian Creed. They were all brief and to the point.

The Apostles Creed has in it only one hundred and five words—you can repeat the whole of it in less than a minute; and the other two are only a trifle longer.

Men were asked in those days, "Do you accept the statements of this creed?" If the man did, he was a Christian; if he did not, then he was a Pagan. And those earnest people thought that they had Scripture for it. "He that believeth and is baptized shall be saved; he that believeth not shall be damned." They stood ready to stake the eternal destiny of a human soul upon his acceptance of or his failure to accept the statements of belief contained in a definite creed.

But in these days we have more than a thousand different creeds, ranging all the way from the Westminster Confession, with its elaborate philosophy of the relations between God and man, to the simplest sort of confession of faith. The Episcopalians have had their thirty-nine Articles of Religion, and the Methodists have their twenty-five Articles.

There is the Augsberg Confession, the Heidelberg Catechism, the Canons of Dort, Calvin's Institutes, and all the other famous standards of belief.

The Baptists and the Disciples, numbering some ten millions of communicants in this country alone, have no creeds at all. They simply refer people to the Bible as their standard of belief, freely according to the individual believer in every case the right of private interpretation. Each local Congregational church has the right to formulate its own creed; and these statements of belief vary widely in their content and phrasing. In the face of these thousands of widely differing interpretations of the eternal verities, how impossible it would be to divide all the people into just two camps, the saved and the lost, on the basis of theological belief!

What then is the test? Is there any valid test? Is there any readily ascertainable difference between those who are Christians and those who are not? What does it mean to be a Christian?

What Is a Christian? 49

In my judgment there is a tremendous difference. The people who are Christians and those who are not are as far apart in purpose, in the spirit which dominates their lives, and in destiny, as are the North Pole and the South Pole. It was the Master himself, you remember, knowing what was in man, who originated that phrase about "the sheep and the goats." In his opinion the man who deliberately and persistently refuses to become a Christian is another kind of an animal altogether. The men who turn their backs on Christianity stand at a long remove from those who are genuine Christians, in their philosophy of life, in the controlling purposes which rule their hearts, and in their prospects for an eternal advance.

What makes that tremendous difference? It all turns in the last analysis upon one's attitude toward a certain person, the Supreme Person in history.

"What think ye of Christ?" What sort of a reaction does his life set up in your life? When he stands before you, do you feel any desire to be like him?

Do you really want him in your life as the dominant directing, transforming influence, taking precedence over all the other influences which may affect your future development? If you take that attitude toward the Supreme Person in the history of the race, then, according to our modern point of view, you are a Christian. It all turns upon one's personal relation to the Supreme Person.

Let me state that principle in even more concrete form. "The word made flesh and dwelling among us full of grace and truth" is still the best word to be had in any field you want to name.

Several years ago we had here in this country a man of forceful and picturesque personality whose name was Theodore Roosevelt. From the Atlantic to the Pacific people were talking about him. They were asking, "What do you think of Roosevelt?" What kind of a man is he? What will be the effect of his influence upon our political and economic life? Will his activities be for our good or for our hurt? How far will the policies

What Is a Christian? 51

which he advocates contribute to our well-being? What think ye of Roosevelt?

Now when that question was asked, it divided people into at least four groups. First, there were those who were undecided. "We hardly know what to think about Roosevelt," they said. They had never seen the man. They did not know him personally. They were not quite sure that they understood his ideas. They felt themselves unable to judge as to whether the net result of his influence would be for the betterment or the injury of the total life of our country. They were on the fence.

In the second place, there were those who were opposed to him. They did not like the man. They did not agree with his principles. They had no use for his ideas about the strenuous life and the big stick, the direct primaries, the recall of judges, the regulation of the trusts, and all the rest of it. They felt sure that he was on the wrong track. They stood ready to oppose him root and branch. "We will not have this man to be president over us," they said, "if we can help ourselves."

In the third place, there were those who gave Roosevelt a conventional support. "What think ye of Roosevelt?" "He is the head of the party," they replied. He is our candidate for the Presidency. Ours not to reason why, ours not to make reply, ours but to vote the straight Republican ticket.

They were "regular"—they took it as it came. It might be McKinley, or it might be Roosevelt; it might be Taft or Harding or Coolidge!—men who stood poles apart in many respects! It mattered not, these men voted with their party whoever might be the candidates.

There were thousands of men who voted for Roosevelt not because they agreed with his principles—they did not agree with some of them at all—but because he was the official head of the party. They were like many of the people who go to symphony concerts. They go not because they like classical music—they do not like it at all, it bores them frightfully—but they think that they ought to like it and that it is the proper thing to do. They attend

What Is a Christian? 53

the concerts therefore and sit through with considerable weariness to the flesh because it is "good form." In like manner there were thousands of men who gave this formal support to Roosevelt.

In the fourth place, there were those who went with him from choice and conviction. They liked the man and they believed thoroughly in his principles. They felt sure that the result of his influence upon our economic and political life would be thoroughly wholesome. They believed that it would insure a purer type of civic life and a more even spread of our prosperity and a more equitable distribution of the good things of life between those who toiled mainly with their hands and those who did their work mainly with their heads. They stood ready to give Roosevelt their support, "good measure, pressed down, shaken together, and running over."

Now that, I take it, is about what we mean in these modern times by being a Christian. You will not of course press my analogy too closely. Not many illustrations will go on all fours—if they get three legs down squarely and firmly, they do well.

To be a Christian means to take and to maintain a certain attitude toward Jesus Christ as the supreme person in history. The man who stands before him in reverent, obedient trust and in heartfelt devotion; the man who is ready to coöperate with him in the realization of his purposes for the race; the man who welcomes the transforming influence of his truth and grace and spirit in his personal life and who desires to give expression to that quality of life in his social relations and activities, becomes by that very mood and bearing a Christian. His attitude toward Christ makes him a Christian no matter what may be his church affiliations or his particular theological beliefs.

The question before the house therefore is that same query propounded of old by the Master himself. "What think ye of Christ?" What is your personal attitude toward this Supreme Person in history?

What Is a Christian?   55

And when that question is asked and is answered, we find the same four groups of people.

First, there are those who are undecided. What think ye of Christ? "We hardly know," they reply. "We haven't thought much about it one way or the other. We haven't even taken the trouble to read carefully what is said about him in this book called the New Testament. We know that people celebrate his birthday every year on the 25th day of December. We usually give presents to the members of our families at that time and have turkey for dinner. And really, that is about as far as we have gotten." They too are on the fence without sufficient strength of mind to get down on either side. That fence is long and broad and along the top of it we find roosting in anemic fashion a multitude which is like the sand of the sea.

In the second place, there are those who are definitely opposed to Christ. They are not all of them wicked or even ignorant and thoughtless people. Some of them have studied the teachings of Christ carefully and they feel that those teachings are impossible. "Very pretty," they say, "in a way but utterly impracticable. Entirely too soft and sentimental for this wicked world where we find ourselves!"

"Nature red in tooth and claw." It is a fight to the finish. The strong win out and the weak go to the wall. The meek have no possible chance of ever inheriting the earth. We cannot get rid of hatred and strife and greed. We cannot eliminate poverty or abolish vice and crime or put an end to war. These things always have been and they always will be. It is human nature and we cannot change human nature by an Act of Congress or by a church resolution. We are descended from the lower animals and there is so much of the ape, the tiger, and the hog left in us that man cannot be expected to live on those high levels portrayed by this gentle dreamer of Nazareth. These people, therefore, quietly put Jesus Christ and his teachings into the waste basket.

What Is a Christian? 57

In the third place, there are those who give Christ a conventional support. They think enough of him to conform outwardly at least to the observances of religion.

They go to church quite regularly when nothing better offers. They know how to behave at church and they make all the moves in the religious game with proper decorum. They give an easy, ready assent to almost any creed statement which is offered them. They take the bread and the wine of the sacrament in a manner thoroughly well-bred. It is a habit they maintain, and as they think, a very good habit.

If we were to follow some of those people to their homes and to their places of employment, we might find them hard and mean, uncharitable and unforgiving. We might find that they had adopted the form of godliness without receiving the power of it or getting into the spirit of it. They move along the religious way as fair weather Christians. When the tide sets strongly toward religious observance, they float in.

When the tide sets strongly away from the Christian mode of conduct, they float out. They have not learned to swim upstream.

When searching temptations come, when exacting obligations are laid upon them, when bitter disappointments arise, when heavy burdens are to be borne, they have not the moral stamina to ascend into the hill of the Lord, and stand there through thick and thin, rain or shine, with clean hands and pure hearts. They haven't it in them. They are merely conventional Christians.

It is not for any one of us to undertake to pin that badge of insincerity upon some one else. It is rather for every one who professes to be a Christian to make thoroughly sure that he is the genuine article himself.

In the fourth place, there are those who are Christians from choice and conviction. What think ye of Christ? They are all ready with their reply. "He spake as never man spake and his words are the words of eternal life. He is the Son of Man, the heir, and the embodiment of all that is essentially and eternally human—and we have no higher aspiration than to be like Him. He is the king of kings—and we desire nothing better than that He should rule our lives. He is 'the Way'—we are trying to walk in it! and 'the Truth'—we accept it—and 'the Life'—God help us to live it! He is Saviour and Lord, and we are persuaded that He is able to keep that which we have committed unto Him against the day of reckoning which is sure to come." This is the attitude taken by those persons who by their bearing toward the Supreme Person become genuinely Christian.

Let me hold before you the pictures of three men who are well known to you all. Look carefully at each one of them in turn—they have something to say on this very point!

Here was Cardinal Mercier of Belgium! He was the saintliest looking man that I have ever seen—and his words and his deeds moved right along with his looks—they were all of a piece. He was a

Roman Catholic and he held certain beliefs which those of us who are Protestants could not accept. He observed a certain mode of worship which, in many of its features, does not appeal to us. But the whole world knew him and honored him as a Christian. His philosophy of life, the spirit which dominated his actions, the wholesome impress of his conduct upon the life of the world through those terrible years of war were such that he was acclaimed everywhere as a genuine Christian. He stood before Jesus Christ in the attitude of reverent, obedient trust and of heartfelt devotion. That was conclusive.

Here was John G. Paton! He was a Scotch Presbyterian. He swallowed the whole Westminster Confession without turning a hair, which Harry Emerson Fosdick with all his splendid Christian devotion could not accept at all when they invited him to join the Presbyterian church.

John G. Paton went out as a missionary to the New Hebrides Islands when the people there were cannibals. He knew at first only two phrases of their language —"God loves you! I love you!" He went around saying that by word and by deed as he ministered to them in unselfish fashion. When he first appeared among them, some of the warriors took up their clubs and were ready to kill him and to eat him. But when they came to feel the spirit of the man, somehow they just could not do it. They laid their clubs down and asked him to baptize them as Christians.

He labored on among them for many years in patience, in kindliness, in unselfish devotion to their welfare. Before he died he had the joy of seeing that cannibalism in those islands was a thing of the past. He saw there a splendid Christian community growing up composed of those men and women who had been savages. He stood before Jesus Christ in reverent obedient trust and heartfelt devotion—and that made him a Christian.

Here was General William Booth, head of the Salvation Army. In his earlier life he was a Wesleyan minister, but he left the Methodist church to organize a more aggressive movement of his own. He developed a noisy mode of worship which does not appeal to most of us. He discarded the two sacraments, baptism and the Lord's Supper, which all other Christians except the Quakers observe. He held certain religious beliefs which I could no more accept than I could believe that two and two make five, or fifty.

But he was a wonderful Christian. He stood out supremely in his generation as the friend of publicans and sinners. What think ye of Christ? "I think he came to seek and to save the lost," William Booth replied, "and I am with him in that undertaking."

When Jesus Christ was here the Pharisees sneered at him because he was "the friend of publicans and sinners." Oxford University conferred the degree of Doctor of Laws upon William Booth for that very reason. He was not a great poet nor a great scientist nor a great statesman, but he was a great Christian. He was the friend of publicans

What Is a Christian? 63

and sinners, and Oxford gave him a LL.D. for it. We are making progress in our appraisals. William Booth stood before Jesus Christ in the attitude of reverent obedient trust and of heart-felt devotion—and the whole world knew him and honored him as a Christian.

How far apart those three men stood when we think of their church affiliations and the creeds they accepted! Cardinal Mercier, a Roman Catholic, John G. Paton, a Scotch Presbyterian, William Booth, head of the Salvation Army! But they were all one "in the unity of the spirit, in the bond of peace, and in righteousness of life."

Those are the things which really count. It is not membership in this organization or in that, it is not the acceptance of this theological statement or of that—these things vary like the color of men's eyes and hair and skin. "With the heart man believeth unto righteousness" and the hearts of those three men all reacted in precisely the same way toward Jesus Christ. They stood together before him in reverent, obedient trust, and in heartfelt devotion—and the world will honor them all as Christians until time is no more.

The central significance of one's attitude toward Christ has been clearly stated by Stanley Jones in his widely read little book, *The Christ of the Indian Road*.

"When I first went to India I was trying to hold a very long line—a line that stretched clear from Genesis to Revelation and on to western civilization and to the Western Christian church. I found myself bobbing up and down that line fighting behind Moses and David and Jesus and Paul and Western civilization and the Christian church.

"I was worried. There was no well defined issue. I found the battle almost invariably being pitched at one of these three places, the Old Testament or Western civilization or the Christian church. I had an ill-defined but instinctive feeling that the heart of the matter was being left out.

"Then I saw that I could and should shorten my line, that I could take my stand at Christ and before that non-Christian world refuse to know anything save Jesus Christ and him crucified. The sheer storm and stress of things had driven me to a place that I could hold.

"Then I saw that there is where I should have been all the time. I saw that the gospel lies in the person of Jesus, that he Himself is the good news, that my one task was to elevate and to present him. My task was simplified.

"But it was not only simplified—it was vitalized. I found that when I was at the place of Jesus, I was every moment upon the vital. Here at this place all the questions in heaven and earth were being settled. He was the one question that settled all others." The determining factor in any man's personal life will be found in his attitude toward the Supreme Person. When we know what he thinks of Christ, not merely in his head but in his heart and in the ordering of his activities, we know where to place him."

Now that personal attitude toward Jesus Christ results in an experience which we call in theological phrase "salvation." The phrase is old but the experience is as fresh as this morning's paper or the dew on the grass.

We are not hearing so much just now in direct terms about "salvation." How many times in the last ten years have you heard a voice from the pulpit or from the pew calling out in so many words, "What must I do to be saved?" There are sections of country where these words would sound strange in these stirring times.

We are compelled to admit that the world at large is not thinking very much these days about being saved. Even among people who take their religion seriously the main emphasis is not upon the thought of eternal blessedness. When Christians meet in conference, they have a great deal to say about the expression of religious impulse in some form of useful service, but very little to say about going to heaven. When even a devout man is on his death bed, the chances are nine to one that he is thinking more about the investments which he has made and the life insurance he carries for the benefit of his wife and children after he is gone, than he is about his own prospects for bliss in some future world.

Now all that apparent disregard for salvation springs, I believe, mainly from a mistaken notion in the minds of many people as to what salvation really is. You may remember that those words "What must I do to be saved? were first uttered in a jail. Two men, Paul and Silas, had been haled before the magistrates on a false charge. They had been swiftly condemned by the rude justice of that early day. Their clothes were stripped off and they were beaten. Then they were turned over to the sheriff who thrust them into the inner prison and made their feet fast in the stocks. The two men, however were undaunted by all that rough treatment—they prayed and sang as if they had been in church, and the other prisoners heard them.

Suddenly at midnight there was a great earthquake. The prison walls were thrown down. The doors were all opened. The bonds of the prisoners were loosed. The sheriff wakened suddenly out of a sound sleep saw what had happened. He supposed that there would be a general jail delivery. Knowing the frightful punishment sometimes meted out by the Roman government in those days to jailers who allowed their prisoners to escape, he drew his sword and was about to kill himself.

Then Paul, one of the two men who had been stripped and beaten, proved himself equal to the emergency. He showed himself, as always, master of the situation. He was not disturbed and he stood there taking thought for the welfare of others. "Do thyself no harm," he called out to the jailer. "We are all here! We are standing by!"

What Is a Christian? 69

The heart of that Philippian jailer was touched to finer issues that night by what he saw and heard and felt. Here were two men untroubled either by nature in one of her most destructive moods, for a great earthquake smashes things, (as I know full well, for I was at San Francisco on the 18th of April, 1906) or by the rough treatment they had received at the hands of men! The two men stood there, serene and undaunted, taking thought for the welfare of their fellow men. "Do thyself no harm—we are all here!"

The jailer had never seen it on that fashion before and he coveted for himself that sense of moral adequacy. He came trembling before Paul and Silas with an appeal for help. "Sirs, what must I do to be saved?" What must I do to have a quality of life like that?

He was not thinking of eternal blessedness in some unseen world. He did not know anything about heaven and hell at that time. He wanted to be like those two men who had shown themselves masters of the situation when the earthquake wrecked the prison.

We are not told all that was said on that occasion—surely a great deal more than appears in this brief summary. But the substance of what the jailer said was this—"What must I do to be saved?" What must I do to be made equal to the moral demands made upon me? And the substance of what Paul said was this—"Believe on the Lord Jesus Christ!" Lay hold upon the highest manifestation which God has made of his redemptive power by entering into personal relations with Jesus Christ. When any man does that in the spirit of a reverent, obedient trust, he will be saved from all that hinders human life in rising to its best estate.

Now that, I take it, is about what we mean by "salvation" in these modern times. Some of you may think that I have put it coldly. Some of you may feel that I have dragged those great words down out of the sky and have given them a meaning which is of the earth earthy.

But I am thoroughly sure that the very essence of salvation is there contained. When any man, facing the demands which are made upon him by his particular situation, does what Paul suggested to that Philippian jailer, he will be linking up his life with that whole system of divine help suggested by the name of Christ. He will enter at once upon that spiritual process which the Scriptures call "being saved." And furthermore, he will be headed straight for all the eternal blessedness which may be in store for any of us.

William James of Harvard, in that widely read book of his, *Varieties of Religious Experience*, undertook to establish two propositions upon the basis of ordinary experience. First, there is something wrong with all of us, morally speaking. Second, the wrongness can only be righted when we make new adjustments with the Higher Powers. And that is exactly what Paul and Silas said that night to the Philippian jailer, only they phrased it differently because they had never been at Harvard.

They are rather particular about the expressions they use at Harvard. We are told that on the day of a great football game between Princeton and Cornell, the Princeton coach received a telegram just before the game was called. When he opened it, it read, "Greetings from Yale! May the best team win!" It was signed by the Yale coach.

Five minutes later another telegram came and when he opened that one, it read, "Greetings from Harvard! May the better team win!"

The Harvard professor said, "There is something wrong with all of us and that wrongness can be righted only as we make new adjustments with the higher powers." The Philippian jailer said, "What must I do to be saved?" And Paul replied, "Believe on the Lord Jesus Christ." It all comes to the same thing. Differences in phrasing, but the same great truth!

What Is a Christian? 73

Let me take up those two points suggested by William James, in discussing with you the question of salvation and in seeking to ascertain exactly what it means to be a Christian.

There is something wrong with every one of us. We have all failed, morally speaking,—you in your way, I in mine, the man across the aisle in his. Not a man here could stand up and say, "I am everything that a man should be—always have been! I have always done those things that please the Father. No unjust, untrue, or unkind word has ever fallen from my lips. These hands have never done anything wrong. These feet have never walked in forbidden paths. No dishonest or unholy purpose has ever found place in my heart."

Put such words on any pair of lips and they sound grotesque. The fact of moral failure is universal—it is written across the whole history of the race in a bold hand.

Here are thousands of people who commit crime and find themselves behind the bars! Here are other thousands who surrender to the coarse sins of the flesh, drunkenness, licentiousness, and the like. Their habits are such that they become liabilities rather than assets to the community. They wreck their own careers and they bring hurt and loss to other lives. Here are other thousands who are moral defectives and delinquents. They may not be guilty of crime but they are so far below par spiritually that they are a menace to the social order. We cannot ignore their existence nor their sore need of some kind of help.

But the wrongness which William James had in mind goes far beyond all that. Here are multitudes of people who are selfish, greedy, inconsiderate of others! Generosity and self-sacrifice, which are imperative for social advance, have small place in their philosophy of life. They are looking out solely for Number One. Here are other multitudes who have become flippant and cynical. When needy souls, beaten and baffled by the hard things of life, turn to these people for help, they have no

What Is a Christian? 75

help to offer. There is no more help in their philosophy of life than would be found in a wet paper bag. Here are other multitudes without faith or hope or love for God in their poor little worlds! Their lives grow thin and weak and dull. Every now and then we read in the morning paper that another one of them has blown his brains out because he felt that there was nothing to live for. He may have been correct from his point of view. Alas for them all! There is something terribly wrong with each one of them.

If keeping out of jail and feathering one's own nest were all that there is to life, we should scarcely need religion. We could do that little job ourselves unaided. Ordinary ability and pleasant surroundings would amply suffice.

But that is not all that there is to life! On every fortunate life there rests a heavy obligation to aid in bringing up the less fortunate messmates at the board of life. The strong are here to bear the infirmities of the weak. To whom much is given, of him will much be required.

"The field is the world and the good seed," which is to make that field fruitful, is to be found, the Master said, in "the children of the kingdom." The hope of the future rests upon those people who have gained some measure of the mind of Christ, who stand ready to shoulder their responsibility and carry on. When any one dismisses his share of that larger obligation with a shrug of the shoulders and a cynical laugh— "no affair of mine"—he shows himself a moral coward and a quitter. There is something fearfully wrong with all such men.

In the second place, the wrongness, whatever form it may take, can only be righted by making those new adjustments to the higher powers. When a man is "converted" as we say, something happens,—something real, something vital, something big with promise. It is like the change which takes place when a trolley car standing there, dark, cold, motionless, makes its connection with the central powerhouse. The trolley car reaches up and lays hold of a mysterious, invisible current of power. Then it is lighted and warmed and moves off upon its way. In like manner any human life which establishes its connections with that Higher Power not ourselves which makes for righteousness, is transformed. "If any man is in Christ"—just as we say a man is "in love" or "in a rage" or "in liquor"—"if any man is in Christ, he is a new creature. Old things are passed away, all things are become new."

Matthew Arnold, as you know, was not in any sense a narrow-minded dogmatist. He was a poet, a philosopher, and a keen observer of human affairs. His free mode of speech, for he never beat around the bush, and his liberal ideas sometimes shocked the pious people of his day. But when he heard Professor Clifford, for example, and other light-hearted unbelievers, attacking the Christian religion, he said this—I quote his words in full because they have the more significance coming as they do from a man of his ability, position, and temperament.

"These are but the crackling fireworks of youthful paradox. One reads it all half-sighing, half-smiling as the clever, confident declamation of hopeless inexperience. Only when we are young and headstrong can we stand by the Sea of Time and instead of listening to the solemn, rhythmic beat of its waves, fill the air with our own whoopings.

"The plain people hear all such talk with impatience and then they flock all the more eagerly to Moody and Sankey. And the plain people are right. As compared with Professor Clifford, Moody and Sankey are masters of the philosophy of history. Men are not mistaken in thinking that Christianity has done them good. They are not mistaken in loving it or in wishing to hear other men talk about it with gratitude and admiration rather than with ridicule and contempt.

"For Christianity"—and here is the nub of Matthew Arnold's whole statement—"Christianity is the greatest and happiest stroke yet made for human perfection."

What must I do to be saved? What must I do to be made morally adequate to the demands upon my life? Believe on the Lord Jesus Christ, Matthew Arnold would say, and William James, and Paul the Apostle! You cannot do anything better for yourself or for the social order where you stand. Make those needed adjustments to the higher powers and the wrongness in you will be righted.

Salvation as the Greek word has it, is soundness, wholeness, the sense of being in some decent measure morally adequate to those demands of duty from which there is no honorable escape. We all have our temptations to overcome, our obligations to meet, our burdens to bear, our share of the common load to shoulder and carry off. All that can best be done by entering into right relations with that Higher Power which is eternal.

"The gospel," as Dean Inge puts it, "is good news, not good advice." It is the good news that God is with us and for us in that quest for life which is life indeed. And to every one who receives that good news and acts upon it, the message becomes the power of God unto moral adequacy.

Here was a man named Wilfred Grenfell! He came many years ago under the influence of Dwight L. Moody. Through Mr. Moody's ministry, he tells us, he came under the influence of the gospel of Christ as he had never experienced it before. It changed his whole career. He was led to devote his unusual intellectual powers, his professional skill as a physician, the force and charm of his personality as a man, to the service of a lot of unfortunate, neglected, forgotten fishermen yonder on the coast of Labrador. He gave himself to them in an unselfish, efficient service which is known and honored today throughout the whole English speaking world.

How did it all come about? How did he come to do it? Why did not some of those ethical culture people, who think that "religion is entirely superfluous," do it? Well, they did not feel like it. It was none of their affair, they said.

What Is a Christian? 81

They thought that they could find pleasanter places to live than Labrador.

Why did not some of those cynical, flippant people go—they go about saying, "There is nothing in religion. Prayer is a farce. The church is a joke. Immortal life is a foolish dream." The need was there,—why did not they go and meet it? Well, they did not feel like it either. The very suggestion that such people would or could do it sounds funny. What would they have had to say to those struggling people in Labrador had they gone? They showed their good sense at least by staying at home.

Wilfred Grenfell went and did it. He is doing it now in glorious fashion. He is a Christian. He had made those adjustments to the Higher Powers which rendered him adequate to the exacting demands of that heroic service.

"The true mark of a saved man," some one has said, "is not that he wants to go to heaven." The true mark of a saved man is that he is willing to go to China or to Labrador, to the battlefields of France or to the slums of a great city, into a hard political fight or to the last dollar of his resources in order to set forward the coming of the kingdom of God on earth. He stands ready to spend and to be spent in order that he may be able to advance the sway and rule of the spirit that was in Christ in all our human affairs.

The saved man has heard his Master say, "Ye are the light of the world—let your light so shine that men may see." He stands there as a candle of the Lord ready to burn to the socket if only light may fall upon the path that goeth forever upward.

Travel up and down the long lanes of human history as you may, you will find this! The only men and women who are really putting the world ahead in those difficult situations which demand moral courage, self-sacrifice, tenacity of purpose, patience, kindliness, spiritual dynamic, are the men and women who have made those necessary adjustments to the higher powers.

They are not undertaking to do it in their own strength—they know full well that they could not. They are not relying solely upon the horizontal forms of energy, sympathy, compassion, neighborly feeling—these are not enough. They are bringing to bear upon those hard tasks the perpendicular forms of energy which are wielded by faith and hope and love for God. They have entered into personal relations with the supreme person in history, Jesus Christ.

It all comes back at last to what Paul said to the Philippian jailer that night when the earthquake was tearing everything to pieces. What must a man do to be made morally adequate to the demands made upon him? Let him believe on the Lord Jesus Christ and thereby make the needed adjustments to the Highest Power known to human experience.

I wonder if we have not had about enough of all this theological strife and contention which sets Christians apart in hostile array! The devil enjoys it—

he likes to see Christians fighting one another when they might be fighting him. But I am sure that it brings no joy to the heart of our Lord, who would have us all become one, even as He and the Father are one. And the greater part of the contention has to do today with matters which after all are only secondary.

The night the Master was betrayed, when he was instituting the Lord's Supper as a perpetual sacrament of remembrance, he named the supreme test of discipleship. It was not to be found in some form of theological opinion, nor in membership in some particular organization, nor in the careful performance of some piece of ritual. "By this shall all men know that ye are my disciples, if ye love one another as I have loved you." Here were the two main moral attitudes to be sought for in all our lives—love for Him and love for one another.

The Master once examined a young man for ordination to the Christian ministry. He asked him but a single question, but because that question was central and decisive he asked it three times over, in order to be sure about it. "Simon, lovest thou me? Lovest thou me? Lovest thou me more than these?" And when the young man's answer came back, clear and firm on that one point, the Master stood ready to ordain him. "Yea Lord, thou knowest that I love thee. Thou knowest that I love thee. Thou knowest all things, thou knowest that I love thee." Three times over he answered straight.

The Master then ordained him to the Christian ministry. He gave him a high commission for an exalted service. "Feed my lambs! Feed my sheep! Tend my sheep." I wonder if in these more recent times we have improved upon the method of the Master in examining candidates for ordination to the Christian ministry?

By love for him, I feel sure that the Master did not mean a mere bit of sentimental feeling or the mere intellectual acceptance of some stoutly orthodox theological statement about his person or the mere making of a formal gesture of worship in his honor. By love for him, I feel sure that He meant the solemn dedication of one's life to the securing of that quality of life which He manifested supremely and is able to reproduce in the hearts of those who love him.

What think ye of Christ, here and now, man to man? It utterly passes my understanding how any intelligent person facing the facts of history for the last nineteen hundred years can fail to think about him in some way and to think seriously.

Here is One who has made his birthday, born though he was in the manger of a stable in an out of the way place, the starting point from which all the leading nations of earth reckon their time. Nineteen Hundred and Twenty-six we say—it is just that long since He was born in Bethlehem of Judea! Here is One who has taken the moral government of the world upon his shoulder as none other ever has! His ideas, principles, and spirit have won for themselves an unapproached primacy in the moral appraisal of the race. Here is One who has shown himself able to meet and satisfy the deepest, the strongest, the holiest impulses of the human heart as no other man ever has in the whole history of mankind.

What think ye of him? What reaction does His life set up in your life? What effect does all this have upon those aspirations, purposes and determinations which are to rule your personal career?

This is what one of our own poets, Richard Watson Gilder, a cultured man of letters in the City of New York, thought about him!

> If Jesus Christ is a man
> And only a man I say,
> Of all mankind I will cleave to him
> And to him I will cleave alway.

> If Jesus Christ is God
> And the only God, I swear
> I will follow him through heaven and hell
> The earth, the sea, the air.

That is what it means to be a Christian! If any man would be his disciple, let him live unselfishly and take up his duty and follow Him.

III

WHAT VALUE HAS RIGHT MOTIVE?

The quality of any action must be judged in two ways! First, by its consequences! We have to consider the effect it has upon the individual himself, upon others who may be affected by it, and upon the interests of society. How does it work?

Second, by the motive and intent which lie back of it! It is not simply what a man does, it is the reason why he does it, the mood and temper in which the thing is done, which determines our estimate of his action. We have to ask, "what?" and also "why?"

For example, if a man does a certain thing with an evil intent, with the purpose of injuring somebody, the fact that it turns out for the advantage of that other person does not make a good action of it. The Lord may cause "the wrath of man to praise him," but the fact still stands that it was "wrath."

Value of Right Motive

When the evil-minded brothers of Joseph sold him as a slave boy to the Midianites to be carried down into Egypt, it was a wicked, cruel action on their part. The fact that it worked out good results did not redeem it. When these men were brought to stand before Joseph after he had become a ruler in Egypt, he said to them, "Ye meant it for evil but God meant it for good." The fact that the Lord had brought good out of their evil conduct did not, however, change the character of their cruel action when they sold their brother into slavery.

On the other hand, if a man does something with the best of intentions but the content of his action is so ill-judged that it does harm, the fact that he "meant well" does not make that a good action. It takes brains to be good in these days—good intentions are not enough. The two elements in right action must go hand in hand, the honest purpose and the wisely ordered conduct—wisely ordered with reference to the consequences which will follow. We must combine what are called the intuitive and the experiential schools of ethics.

The law of the land recognizes that fact. Here are four men each one of whom has killed another man. The first man did it deliberately in cold blood. He poisoned his victim, or he lay in wait for him in the dark and shot him down, or he crept up behind him and stabbed him to the heart. This is "murder in the first degree" and in many states it is punishable by death. In all states it stands as the gravest crime in the calendar.

The second man was engaged in a quarrel. In the heat of passion or under some sudden provocation, with no previously cherished purposes of murder, he did intentionally kill his man. We call that "murder in the second degree" and it is punishable by a sentence less severe.

The third man had no intention of killing anybody, but he was doing that which was unlawful and criminally careless. He may have been driving an automobile through the streets with a reckless disregard for the safety of others. He may have been clearing off rubbish from the top of a high building, throwing down bricks or boards into the street where people were likely to be passing. He may have been discharging a gun in a place where other people were likely to be injured. In any one of those ways he may have killed some one. We call that "manslaughter" and here the penalty is even less severe.

The fourth man was not doing anything unlawful or even reckless. He may have been chopping wood when his axe head flew off of the handle and killed some innocent bystander. He may have tripped when he was carrying a loaded gun—the gun was discharged and killed the man who was walking ahead. He may, by some unfortunate accident in industry have actually killed another. This is not a crime at all—it is "accidental homicide"—and it is not punishable by law.

In every one of these instances the consequences were the same—in each case the man's action resulted in the taking of human life. But because of the varying moods and tempers in which the deed was done, society places a different appraisal upon each one of those actions.

The Master of all the higher values in life knew this full well and he once told a short story to illustrate the significance and value of right motives. There was a certain planter who had a vineyard. The grapes were ripe and ready to be picked. The householder went out to hire men for his vineyard.

The ordinary working day at that time was twelve hours in length,—it lasted from six o'clock in the morning until six o'clock at night. It was a situation where the steel trust of a few years ago would have felt thoroughly at home. This man went out early in the morning and hired men to work in his vineyard at a shilling a day. The bargain was made and agreed to by both

Value of Right Motive 93

parties and the men went to work at six o'clock in the morning.

The owner of the vineyard went out again at nine o'clock and, at twelve o'clock, and at three o'clock in the afternoon. On each one of those occasions he saw men standing idle, and in each case, he said to them, "Go work in my vineyard and whatever is right, you will receive." Nothing was said in any case as to the amount of the wage to be paid, but the men entered at once upon their service.

The employer went out finally at five o'clock, within an hour of quitting time, and said to certain men, "Why stand ye here all the day idle?" They replied, "Because no man hath hired us." He said to them, "Go ye also into the vineyard and whatsoever is right, you will receive." They promptly went to work to accomplish what they could in that single hour which remained.

When six o'clock came, the men all came in to be paid off. Those who were hired at five o'clock, who had worked only an hour, received a shilling apiece. Likewise the men who had worked three hours or six hours or nine hours received also a shilling apiece. Last of all the men who had been at work since six o'clock in the morning came, expecting that they would receive much more. Having worked for the full twelve hours they felt that they should receive twelve times as much as did the men who had worked but one hour. But they too received a shilling apiece according to the bargain which they had made earlier in the day.

Then they set up a howl of protest. "These men have wrought but one hour and thou hast made them equal unto us who have borne the heat and burden of the day."

Then the employer said to them, "I do thee no wrong. Didst thou not agree with me for a shilling a day?" You made your bargain—now stand to it man-fashion!

It is a most unlikely story! No one could do business on any such basis. Imagine the results in a factory or a mill where the superintendent undertook to pay the men who were working ten hours a day or eight hours a day exactly the same wage which he paid men who were doing the same work but were putting in only one hour a day! We would have industrial unrest in that factory raised to the *nth* degree. The I. W. W.'S would come and tear the place down before a week had passed.

But the Master was not teaching economics—he was teaching morals. He was not outlining an industrial program, he was indicating the importance of right motive. The point of his story was this—a small amount of work done in the right spirit has more value in it, in the eyes of him who looks not merely upon the outward performance but upon the heart, not merely upon achievement but upon the underlying purpose, than a much larger amount of work has where it is done in the wrong mood.

The men who do their work in the bargaining spirit, working always with their eyes on the clock, waiting constantly for the whistle to blow, seeking to get through each day with as little effort as possible without actually losing their jobs, working merely for the wages they receive—all these men receive much less in proportion than do those men who do their work faithfully not knowing always just what they will receive. And that is sound moral teaching every day in the week and in every country the sun shines on. The bargaining spirit is fatal to the highest achievement in any field you want to name. It lacks the right motive.

This short story came swiftly upon the heels of an unhappy question asked by Peter. "Master, we have left all and followed thee—what shall we have therefore?" What are we going to get out of it? How much is there in it for us?

Peter belonged to that race which has shown itself unusually thrifty and on this occasion he seems to have had his eye on the main chance. He too was looking out for Number One with the idea that if he did not, nobody would. "We have left all to follow thee,—what shall we have therefore?"

We are sorry Peter said it. It strikes the wrong note. The man who is serving God for what he can get out of it is not serving him at all. He is simply transacting a little business with the Lord. The man who follows Christ with a basket on his arm to gather up the loaves and the fishes as he goes along, may get something to eat, but man does not live by bread alone.

The young man who sends some flowers to a young lady, hoping that she will invite him to that dinner party or dance which she is planning to give in a week or two, is not showing her any courtesy. He is merely undertaking to do a little social business with the young lady. The commercial spirit stains whatever it touches whenever it invades the realm of good manners or good morals. It is the friendly, uncalculating spirit which clothes any action with beauty.

The finest forms of satisfaction cannot be gotten for pay. The man who goes out to secure them for cash down in a bargaining spirit, so many shillings for so much of the thing desired, will come back empty-handed and empty hearted. The fine friendship of one man for another, the woman's kiss of affection, the mother's attachment to her children, the scholar's devotion to research, the patriot's love for his country—these high values cannot be gotten for cash. They are not bought and sold as if they were meat and potatoes. The man who tries to purchase friendship or a woman's affection for money receives only a sorry counterfeit. These things are all given away—in the very nature of the case they have to be. The underlying motive in each case is not mercenary.

Here is a familiar child's story which throws light on that principle! There was a boy once whose name was Richard. His boy friends never called him that—they called him "Dick." His father called him "Dick" except when he was about to reprove him for some wrongdoing. Whenever his father said, "Now Richard," Dick knew what was coming. But his mother always called him

Value of Right Motive

"Richard" because she felt that it would sound better when he grew up and became a man. She wished to have it known that he had always borne that name.

This boy had an unhappy feeling that he was being asked to do more than his share of the family chores. He felt abused and "put upon." One morning when his mother came to the breakfast table she found a slip of paper by her plate. When she took it up and read it, she found this:

Mother,
  owes Dick

For sweeping the front walk............$	.20
For bringing up wood.................	.25
For taking her letters to the box........	.15
For going on errands to the grocery.....	.30
Total.......................$	.90

His mother read it through carefully, got up and went for her purse and handed Richard ninety cents.

He thanked her and put the money in his pocket. He was highly pleased—he had found a new way to get pocket money. He was thinking of the ice cream sodas and the movie tickets and the other forms of satisfaction which were now within his reach. When a ten year old boy has ninety cents in his pocket to be spent as he pleases, he feels that he has the world by the tail.

He had a beautiful time that day, but the next morning when he came to the breakfast table he found a piece of paper by his plate. He took it up and read it and found this:

Richard
    owes Mother
For mending his clothes when he tore
 them playing football.............. Nothing
For nursing him when he had the measles Nothing
For helping him with his lessons....... Nothing
For putting up his lunch for the Boy
 Scout picnic..................... Nothing
          ―――――
    Total.................... Nothing

He put the paper in his pocket and all that day he was thinking about it off and on. He was thinking about how much his mother had done for him, how unselfish she had been and yet she had never sent in a bill. On the con-

Value of Right Motive 101

trary here was a complete discharge from all his obligations.

That night when he was ready for bed, he threw his arms around her neck and said, "Mother, I want to do things for you for nothing."

It is only a child's story, but the whole psychology of right motive is there contained. The quality of any action is not to be measured by the size of it, but by the spirit of it.

"Why should I be religious?" some man asks. What would religion do for me? Why should I go to church? What would I get out of it?

Well, not very much—hardly anything in fact if the man goes in that mood. If he stands yonder at the door of the church bargaining with the deacons and with the Lord as to how much he will get back for the time he spends in God's house and for the money he drops into the plate, he might just as well stay out. Unless he comes in with finer motives, offering in an ungrudging spirit a reverent, obedient trust to the One above, and good will, friendliness, and kindly service to his fellows, it is not worth his while to come at all.

The bargaining spirit here as everywhere is fatal. The smallest amount of worship or of kindly action offered in the right mood is of more worth than a vast array of performance put forth in the spirit of the hireling. This is the teaching of that parable of the hours where the men who went to work at five o'clock in the afternoon without knowing just how much they were to get out of it, received as much as did the men who had made a bargain and then had worked from six o'clock in the morning until six o'clock at night.

There are some things which one can do after a fashion even if his motives are not high and even though his heart may not be in his work. He can break rock in that spirit—even though he is mad all over, he may do his work well. He may even play a little game with himself by imagining that all those rocks

Value of Right Motive 103

are people whom he does not like. In that event his blows will be all the harder.

He may turn the grindstone even though he has no more sense of sympathy in his breast than the grindstone has. The mood of the man who turns the grindstone does not permeate the grindstone. It will sharpen the scythe just as rapidly as if the man were rejoicing in his work while he turned the crank.

But there are other things which a man cannot do at all if his motives are not right. If he is teaching a room full of boys and girls; if he is managing a shop full of artisans as a foreman or a superintendent; if he is selling goods to customers, who will not buy unless they are pleased; if he has in his care the lives or the property of a lot of people because he is employed on a railroad; if he is a lawyer seeking to have justice prevail among litigants, or a doctor or a nurse caring for the sick, or a minister preaching the gospel, then the mood and the motives which lie back of his action are of supreme importance. The narrow, mercenary, bargaining spirit in any one of these lines of action will mean defeat.

Here is the big, solid social order enfolding us all! It gives a certain answer to every one who applies. It "reacts" upon him as we say. He gets a certain rebound from it as the years come and go.

One set of people make their approach in a greedy, grasping spirit. Some of them in high station, some of them in low—this spirit is not the monopoly of any one class. Another set of people make their approach in a friendly, trustful, coöperative spirit—these people also are found scattered here and there all the way up and down the social scale. Which class gets the most out of life?

We all know! "With the same measure they mete it out, it is measured back to them." I would almost say that in the long run, the second group of people will get more money—they will certainly get more satisfaction, more of the gratitude and esteem of their fellows, more peace and joy in life.

Value of Right Motive

There was a certain stingy old chap once who attended church very regularly. He had been grabbing everything within reach with both hands and he was rich. He had never entered into the joy of giving. It required a major operation with ether and surgical instruments to get money out of his pockets for any kind of a benevolent offering.

One Sunday the minister of the church he attended preached a powerful sermon from the text, "It is more blessed to give than to receive." The preacher actually caused a bit of sap to run in that dry old log sitting there stiffly in his pew. He closed his sermon by picturing the blessed rewards in store for the generous. When the service was over and that stingy man passed out of the church the people noticed that he stopped and gave a penny apiece to a dozen old beggar women who had gathered about the door of the church. Then one of the deacons said to another, "Look there! Mr. Thrifty thinks that he is purchasing a penny's worth of Paradise for himself."

When we are at our best, the grasping, calculating spirit is not in evidence. There is another sort of motive altogether in command.

> "Then only the Master shall praise us,
>   And only the Master shall blame,
> And no one shall work for money
>   And no one shall work for fame.
> But each for the joy of the working
>   And each in his separate star
> Shall draw the thing as he sees it,
>   For the God of things as they are."

How much depends upon one's philosophy of life as it finds expression in the ordering of his various activities! Here are certain beliefs, hopes, fears, which profoundly influence all our determinations. They furnish us more august sanctions for righteousness. They offer more powerful deterrents from evil. They open up fresh sources of motive and stimulus. They steady and strengthen the will. They give reach and grasp to our aspirations.

The earth is another sort of place altogether when it is seen to have a

Value of Right Motive

sky above it. Human life is another thing altogether when it is viewed as stretching on into a future, unknown indeed, but alluring in its power of appeal. It is tomorrow even more than yesterday which determines our action today—and if there be an unending series of tomorrows awaiting us, then how mighty becomes their appeal!

There are three main outstanding impulses which are steadily yielding their respective supplies of motive power for the serious business of living. The desire to get, the wish to keep, the willingness to share! You will find those forms of motive woven into the whole social order which enfolds us.

Let me read you another short story, which throws light upon all three of these forms of motive—it is taken from the best book of short stories to be found anywhere in print!

A certain lawyer stood up testing him and said, "Master, what shall I do to inherit eternal life?"

Jesus said to him "What is written in the law? How readest thou?"

He answering said, "Thou shalt love the Lord thy God with all thy heart and thy neighbor as thyself."

Jesus said, "Thou hast answered right. This do and thou shalt live."

But wishing to justify himself, he said, "And who is my neighbor?"

Jesus answered, "A certain man went down from Jerusalem to Jericho and fell among thieves. They stripped him of his raiment, wounded him, and departed leaving him half dead.

"By chance there came down a certain priest that way and when he saw him passed by on the other side. Likewise a Levite, when he was at the place came and looked on him and passed by on the other side. But a certain Samaritan, as he journeyed, came where he was and when he saw him he had compassion on him. He went to him and bound up his wounds, pouring in oil and wine. He set him on his own beast and brought him to an inn and took care of him.

"And on the morrow when he departed he took out two shillings, and gave them to the host and said, 'Take care of him and whatsoever thou spendest more, when I come again I will repay thee.' Which now of these three thinkest thou was neighbor unto him that fell among the thieves?"

The lawyer answered, "He that showed mercy on him."

Jesus said to him, "Go and do thou likewise."

Value of Right Motive

When that man went down from Jerusalem to Jericho he encountered three different types of people. First the robbers, then the priest and the Levite, and then the Samaritan. In a way they represent the people we all meet and they also suggest those three different forms of motive which I have just named, the desire to get, the wish to keep, and the willingness to share. Let me hold the pictures of those men before you again—look at each one of them in turn! They have something to say on this very point!

First, the robbers! Every man in that group had a certain philosophy of life. It was this—"What's yours is mine, I'll take it." They fell upon that traveler, stripped him of his raiment, wounded him, took all he had and departed, leaving him half dead. They believed in the good old rule, the simple plan that he should take who has the power and he should keep who can. They did not use the King James version of the scriptures. Their translation of the Golden Rule read like this—"Do the other fellow before he has a chance to do you." What's yours is mine—Hands up!—I will take it!

Now there are a great many different ways of robbing people. Differences of administration but the same evil purpose. Those men on the Jericho road did it in a knock down fight. The bank robber does it at the point of a pistol. The sneak thief does it by slipping his hand into the pocket where you carry your purse or your watch when you are not looking. The loan shark does it by taking advantage of the necessities of poor people and charging them a rate of interest which is thievish. Diversity of operation, yet it is all stealing!

But all those fellows are amateurs—their methods are crude and clumsy. We send them to state's prison whenever they are caught. There are finer ways of robbing people. The Jericho road is much longer than those thirty miles which stretch between Jerusalem and the Jordan Valley. It reaches clear round the globe—it goes everywhere.

Value of Right Motive 111

On that road we see a great many men who do not look like robbers—they are well-dressed, respectable-looking people like ourselves. But they are making gain by exploiting the weak. They often pay wages which are less than equitable. They work their employees an unreasonable number of hours. They maintain conditions in their mills and their mines which are unsanitary and dangerous. They are sometimes industrial slackers who do not give a fair day's work for a fair day's pay—they waste the time and the material for which their employers have paid and thereby increase the cost of the product for us all. They sometimes profit from lying advertisements, or from political graft. They "pile on all the traffic will bear," regardless, because it means more profit. What do you call that? Are they not robbers too?

One man of evil purpose kills another with a gun or a knife in five minutes. Another man kills people in five years with unsanitary tenements, with adulterated food, with unfair labor conditions.

In either case it is murder in the eyes of Him who knows. It takes life.

One man robs people at the point of a gun. Another man robs them by economic methods which are unsocial and unjust. In either case it is stealing. Several years ago a hungry tramp stole a ham one night from a freight car on the railroad. He was caught the next day with the ham under his arm and he was sent to prison, as he should have been. It is wrong to steal hams. That same winter a group of men, engaged in high finance, by manipulating the stock stole the railroad. But when they were caught with the railroad under their arms, they were not sent to prison. How about that?

How about those men who profit from child labor, trading upon the toil of little people who ought to be at school or playing in the open air? How about those men who fatten upon the labor of women who are striving to make a bare living with their needles? How about those men who see to it that the farmer gets a low price for that which

Value of Right Motive 113

his land produces, yet when you and I come to consume that produce we pay a high price for it? The big, wide margin between goes mainly into the pockets of men who do not produce anything—they trade upon what other men produce. How about those men who manufacture articles which are for sale rather than for use! The articles look well long enough to be sold but the material is poor, the workmanship worse, and their utility slight.

How about all those people? Would you not call their action robbery? I have read the Bible through a good many times and I am fairly familiar with the dictionary. I know of no other word to be applied to it but "stealing." They are taking what does not belong to them. When any man takes from another or from society that for which he has not given a just equivalent, either in money or in service rendered by the labor of hand or of brain, he is stealing. What's yours is mine—I'll take it. That is their philosophy of life, and a wicked philosophy it is.

In the second place this man on the road to Jericho encountered the Priest and the Levite. Here was our common humanity lying at the roadside wounded and helpless! By chance there came along a certain priest. When he saw that bit of human need, he said to himself: "No affair of mine! I did not rob the man. Never robbed anybody in my life! It is his own fault—careless of him to have been traveling alone in this region where brigands lurk among the rocks." Thus he excused himself from all responsibility in the matter and passed by on the other side.

Then a Levite came along. He was not quite so brutally cold and selfish as the Priest. "He came and looked upon" the man. He may have asked his name in case the poor fellow had partially regained consciousness. He probably inquired how many robbers there were and how much of his money they got and if he was suffering much pain from those wounds in his head. Then having gotten all the statistics—having made a survey so to speak—and

Value of Right Motive 115

having expressed his regret that such things were allowed to happen in this wicked world he too passed by on the other side. Those two men also had their philosophy of life—it was this, "What's mine is my own—I'll keep it."

They were very respectable men, no doubt, like ourselves. They were religious men, we know. It was the Priest's business to preach religion in the temple service just as I do every Sunday. It was the Levite's business to sing religion in the temple service. The Levites made up the choir in the Jewish church. It is a thousand pities that the Priest and the Levite were not practicing their religion that day on the Jericho road. It would have immortalized them. Everybody in Christendom knows the Good Samaritan, and his action on that occasion has made him more popular than Santa Claus. But the Priest and the Levite have been kicked and cuffed from that day to this. "What's mine is my own, I'll keep it," is not a philosophy of life which makes friends.

Yet what a lot of it there is! The Priest and the Levite represent a multitude, which no man can number, of all nations and peoples and kindreds and tongues. They stand off looking at these bits of human need, thoughtless, careless, selfish as pigs. They are always turning their faces away from human need and passing by on the other side.

When they see a woman left a widow with a bunch of little mouths to be fed, or boys and girls living on oatmeal and crackers in their struggle for an education, or good causes of all sorts held back and crippled for lack of support, these self-centered people never turn a hair. "What's mine is my own! Worked hard for it! Always paid my own way a hundred cents on the dollar. I am not giving any of it away for the sake of sentiment. I'll keep it." They are stingy, forgetting apparently what Jesus said about the fate of the stingy.

"The Levite came and looked upon" the wounded man—and these stingy people are willing oftentimes to do that much. They rather enjoy looking at human need—they often feel that they have been doing their duty when they were merely looking at it or hearing about it. When they read the *Survey* regularly and listen to wise lectures on "scientific charity," when they attend wonderful conferences on "charities and corrections," and hear stirring addresses by social reformers who are ready to reconstruct the whole social order overnight, when they go to see plays like "The Fool" and cry a little, they often think that they must have been making considerable moral progress because they have felt so badly about the need of the world. People whose sympathies are not sufficiently exercised by being brought into contact with the painful realities of life frequently enjoy a little extra rubbing and moral massage. Then they cross over and pass by on the other side.

It is frightfully easy for college students to become thoroughly selfish. They have so much done for them by those who love them, by those who are paid to minister to their well-being, and by those who have created splendid endowments for their benefit, that they sometimes feel that they must be the center of the whole solar system and that the sun, moon, and stars revolve mainly for their enjoyment. High privileges grow around them so thick and fast that they overlook the obligations which privilege entails. "To whom much is given, of him will much be required!"

What high praise was given to those early Christians at Jerusalem! "No man said that any of the things that he possessed were his own." They were all held in trust. Those men were good stewards of the values under their control and they used them in the spirit of consecration to ends higher than personal advantage.

Here is a five dollar bill which I happen to have. Is it my own to do with as I like? I did not steal it—I earned it in my profession. But into the creation of that bit of value before it came into the possession of Yale University to be paid to me for service rendered, there went the labor of some other man's hand or brain. It is an expression of life; it is stored up life. If I should use it for some evil purpose or in some thoughtless piece of self-indulgence, I should be wronging the man who helped to create that bit of value and I should be wronging those interests which in its modest way it might be made to serve. It is not my own to do with as I like. The Priest and the Levite were all astray in their philosophy of life. The world cannot move along with the idea that what is mine is my own,—I will keep it. It is the devil's philosophy of life.

In the third place, this man on the Jericho road had still another experience. "A certain Samaritan as he journeyed came where he was" and when he saw that bit of human need "he was moved with compassion." He said to himself, "I did not rob the man, but the fact that I am here, sound and well with money in my purse, while he lies there helpless, creates an obligation. I am the only man in sight to do anything about it. It is up to me—it is my job!"

He tore off strips from his flowing Oriental garment and bound up the man's wounds. "He poured in oil and wine," which the traveler in that country usually carries with him for his lunch. A little oil on the bandages to make them soft and a little wine down the man's throat to revive him, for he was "half dead"! He got him up "and set him on his own beast." He was willing to get off and walk for a time so that a needier man might ride to a place of safety. He got him to an inn and took care of him and saved his life. He too had his philosophy of life—it was this! "What's mine is ours—we'll share it."

"The man on horseback," not in the sinister sense in which that phrase is commonly used but in the sense that nearly every man is mounted on some advantages which might be used upon occasion to serve a needier life. The Samaritan was mounted that day on a small Syrian donkey such as they use

Value of Right Motive 121

in that country. It was not much of a beast to look at, but he used it to save a man's life.

Most of us are mounted. We may not be riding in a coach and six or in a Pierce Arrow limousine, but we have at least a Syrian donkey or a Ford car under us. We have money in our purses —we haven't been robbed. We have homes, not all of them palaces of luxury, but places of comfort. We have intelligence, not as much perhaps as Solomon or President Eliot of Harvard, but enough to get along. We have some measure of goodness—nothing prancing or showy, but like the Samaritan's donkey, plain, useful, everyday goodness. And here we are on the Jericho road with human need scattered along every mile of it! What are we going to do about it? Are we ready to accept that third philosophy of life? "What's mine is ours—it is to be shared with the less fortunate."

Any healthy man with two hands and two feet and one head with more or less in it, can ride his donkey from Jericho clear up to the New Jerusalem without robbing anybody or wounding anybody on the road, simply riding and letting ride. It is as easy as rolling off a log. But that is not the way to inherit eternal life, Jesus said to the lawyer whose question called out this familiar parable. The man who rides up to the gate of heaven mounted on his own advantages, without having used those advantages along the way to aid helpless people to make their way to the gate of heaven, will find that gate shut. It does not open to that sort of an approach. The very essence of eternal life, the whole spirit of the Christian religion, lies in a certain willingness to get down off of some advantages which rightfully belong to us in order to set some helpless life upon them that he too may rise. What's mine is ours!

This is the doctrine Paul preached and there is none better. It is acceptable to the Fundamentalist and also to the Modernist. William Jennings Bryan believed in it and Harry Emerson Fosdick

VALUE OF RIGHT MOTIVE 123

preaches it every Sunday. It is good, sound doctrine at Dayton, Tennessee, or at Princeton, or in Boston. "Look not every man on his own things but every man also on the things of others. Have this mind in you which was also in Christ Jesus! He being in the form of God thought it not a prize to be grasped to be on an equality with God. But he made himself of no reputation, took upon him the form of a servant, and was made in the likeness of men. And being found in fashion as a man, he became obedient unto the death of the cross."

He got off and came down that he might give himself for us in that redemptive love and self-sacrifice which would bring us to the Father. "Wherefore God hath highly exalted him and hath given him a name which is above every name." In that hour when "God so loved the world" as to give his only begotten Son, Jesus said, "What is mine is ours, we will share it." That made him the Savior. It is that philosophy of life which is to save the world.

One of our own poets puts it in the mouth of Christ in his "Vision of Sir Launfal."

> "Not what we give, but what we share,
> For the gift without the giver is bare:
> Who gives himself with his alms feeds three,
> Himself, his hungering neighbor and me."

What's mine is ours, we'll share it! If that philosophy of life is carried out along the Jericho road and wrought into the daily round of duty, it will finally lift that whole region up to the style and manners of the New Jerusalem at its best.

There is a lovely story here in the Old Testament. It may not be literal and exact history—perhaps it is only a parable or a bit of folklore. I would not dogmatize on that point. There was a famine in Syria and the people were dying right and left from starvation. There was a poor widow who had reached the end of her resources—she did not know where the next meal was coming from. She had a little meal at the bottom of her barrel and a little oil in a cruse. She was about to mix it up and bake a little cake for herself and her son and they would eat it; and then, she supposed that they would die as others were dying from starvation.

But that very day there came to her home a prophet of the Lord. He asked her for something to eat. Poor and desperate though she was she shared with him her last morsel of food. The grateful prophet stayed on in her house, and somehow, the story says, so long as she continued to share with him what she had, she continued to find meal in that barrel and oil in that cruse. "She and he and her son did eat from it many days and the barrel of meal wasted not neither did the cruse of oil fail."

Call it poetry or call it prose, as you like, there is a great truth there! So long as she said to those who were even more needy than herself, "What's mine is ours, we'll share it," the supplies held out.

We have been thinking of these three philosophies of life up to this point purely in personal terms. Before we go, let me broaden the scope of their application. The desire to get, the wish to keep, and the willingness to share are forms of motive which have a vast and far-reaching social significance for these troubled times on which we have fallen.

We would all agree that no strong nation has the right to say to a weaker nation "What's yours is mine, I'll take it." When any nation does that by military force, it becomes a thief and a robber. Sooner or later it will learn the meaning of that terrible judgment uttered by the Lord. "The wicked shall be turned into hell and all the nations that forget God." We have seen that very principle worked out in our own day. The way of selfish aggression is hard.

We would all agree that no nation has the right to say "What's mine is my own, I'll keep it for myself." How wonderfully, for example, this nation has been blessed! A position of unique advantage between two great oceans! A magnificent array of wide and varied re-

Value of Right Motive 127

sources! A climate unsurpassed for active industry! A people strong, capable, aspiring, made up from the blending of the more forceful elements in many races! An honorable history affording inspiration to all of us who stand in that goodly succession! We too might say what Israel said of herself in the days of her glory, "What nation hath God so nigh unto them, as the Lord our God is unto us in all things that we call upon him for!"

We have not been beaten and robbed in the last ten years as great sections of Europe have been by a disaster unspeakable. We have not suffered from the devastating influences of war as France and Belgium, Russia and Great Britain, Germany and Austria and Italy have suffered. We are not helpless and half-dead. The economists tell us that the wealth of this country at the present time amounts to fifty per cent more than the wealth of Great Britain and France, Germany and Italy all combined. Here we are on the Jericho road, strong and rich, joyous and hopeful!

What are we going to do about it? Are we going to stand aloof from those intricate, baffling problems in Europe and say, "No affair of ours! We did not bring on the war." Are we going to say, as I heard a well-known United States Senator, then an aspirant for the Presidency, say in cynical fashion yonder in Carnegie Hall, New York, "Let the people of this country attend strictly to their own business, and let Europe stew in her own juice"?

Are we going to say that? Do we dare, as children of Him who holds all the nations in the hollow of his hand, to stand up in His presence and utter any such selfish, heartless, godless word? How could this nation whose God is the Lord utter such blasphemy against the divine purpose for all mankind?

What then shall we say? I am not wise enough to stand here at the close of these lectures and hand out to you in half a dozen neat formulas all the various steps to be taken by this country in meeting our full share of responsibility for the peace and good order of the world.

Value of Right Motive

I am not a statesman. But this I do say —where there is a will there's a way. And where there is the right sort of will on the part of a strong, intelligent, aspiring people, the right sort of way can always be found. It is for the United States of America to say, "What is mine is ours, to be shared in that wider sense of international obligation." That obligation we must accept, and that obligation, by the grace of God, we must meet in full.

www.ingramcontent.com/pod-product-compliance
Lightning Source LLC
Chambersburg PA
CBHW030116010526
44116CB00005B/266